Nature and You

Vaishnavi Joshi

Presentation by *BookLeaf Publishing*

Web: www.bookleafpub.com

E-mail: info@bookleafpub.com

ISBN: 9789363317901

First edition 2024

I dedicate "NATURE AND YOU" to my family and friends, especially my mini version—my Son! Hope you learn to read soon and go through this work of your Mumma, my baby, truly wish you like it!

ACKNOWLEDGEMENT

I would like to acknowledge each and every person I have been related to so far in my life. Each person has taught me something more about myself that makes me reflect and write in retrospect to express my reflections about self. I have written this book during my maternity break with my 9-month-old baby boy which makes this extremely special and memorable.

I truly hope you all—my readers—like this book. Thanks for taking out time and choosing to read my book. I would love to know more about your reading experience, reach out to me at: authorvaishnavijoshi@gmail.com

PREFACE

Welcome to "Nature and You," a collection of 51 poems that delve into the profound relationship between us and the natural world. As you journey through these verses, I invite you to contemplate the timeless wisdom that surrounds us in nature and to consider its relevance to our lives as human beings.

In crafting these poems, I found myself drawn to the intricate tapestry of life that exists beyond the confines of human civilization. I observed the rhythms of the seasons, the harmony of ecosystems, and the resilience of the natural world. Through these observations, I came to a simple yet profound realisation: the principles that govern life in nature are not exclusive to any particular species, but are universal truths that resonate across all living beings on Earth.

Each poem in this collection is a testament to this interconnectedness, exploring themes of growth, emotions, harmony, and beauty of nature. From the gentle sway of a tree in the breeze to the relentless flow of a river carving its path through the landscape, nature speaks to us in myriad ways, offering guidance and wisdom to those who pause to listen.

INDEX

MOTHER NATURE

Look around you,
Look within you…

Look above you,
Look beneath you…

What have you gained in life so far?
What is most abundant and priceless so far?

What keeps you sane and doesn't let you fail?
Who can just read your eyes and rightly tell?

Who loves you right from the moment you were
created?
For whom you are always a winner, even if in
reality defeated?

Whose love does not change as you evolve
through life?
Who risks her everything and gives you life?

There is only one and there cannot be another,
She is Mother Nature, Mother Earth and
Mother…

All of them exist only for you,
Nothing makes them happier than nourishing
you…

They gave you all they had yet keep giving you
everything they store,
Never expect you to pay back nor check if you
love them less or more…

Such is a mother's love, limitless and infinite,
If you can't love them equally back, at least treat
them right…

We are because they are,
We survive because they are…

So let's do our part and reciprocate,
If you can't create, at least protect…

Preserve them, conserve them,
Imitate them, nurture them…

Because the world thrives only on their love and
care,
Replenish them back with love and do your
share!!!

BE YOU

Many were here before me,
Many will be here after me…

But I am not them,
I am "me"...

Tomorrow shall always bring better successors,
Just as I came yesterday, over my
predecessors…

Existence is all about the life lessons I gain,
Learned through inexperience, innocence and
pain…

Life is worth every second spent here honestly,
Happiest when I play the true version of "Me"
modestly!!!

Hence I neither mask, nor pretend, just be...
And effortlessly allow the World to see,

Most incredible creation of God I will be,
When I genuinely embrace the original ME!

DREAM

What is truth and what is lie,
Ultimately it's only a perception we stand by...

Our dreams are made of unfiltered emotions,
Driven by ambitions, fears and unsaid
intentions...

Such are dreams, seen with closed eyes,
There is another kind too, seen with open eyes...
Which are set to become goals of lives..

For some, dreams and goals are clear,
For some, they keep changing forever...

Dreams make every life hopeful,
A struggle fulfilling a dream, is considered
fruitful...

Life is all about dreaming and manifesting,
So keep dreaming, for what are you waiting?

Dream of witnessing spectacular rainbows,
Dream of reaching new heights after hitting
lows…

Dream of a bright sunny day after rains,
Dream of inner satisfaction after pains…

Dream of a life you feel you have made the most
of,
Dream of empowering every person you truly
care of…

Dream of everlasting wellness and heartfelt
laughter,
Dream of achieving most of many things you are
persistently after…

All dreams won't be fulfilled, they are not meant
to be,
But they make life worth living in full force, as
it should be…

Never stop trying, never say never,
You will always find time to chase, what you
truly cared for forever!

Like every caterpillar dreams to be a butterfly
one day,
Every migratory bird dreams of returning to
homeland one day…

So does every tamed animal dream of returning
to the forest one day,
And every caring human combating pollution,
dreams of restoring original pure nature one day!

IMPRESSIONS

For almost each moment everyday,
You impact everyone, everything around in a
way…

Knowingly or unknowingly, you give them
reasons,
to be happy or sad or remember it for all
seasons…

Be the reason for someone's happiness today,
before you blame, try to first understand today…

Admire the beauty of prolific nature around,
don't forget to put smiles on faces that
surround…

Make sure the impact and impressions you
leave,
on other's hearts, only make them believe…

that world is full of magic, happiness and bliss, leave only treasurable impressions and spread peace!

ETERNAL RELATIONSHIPS

Never seen a relationship more rhythmic and hit,
as the one between waves of water and sand
surrounding it…

Waves keep on rising, hitting the shore,
then returning back to the ocean for more…

And in this journey, sand stands still,
quietly accompanying, or moving at wave's
will…

When a wave hits the shore, it conceals the
existence of land…
Along with it washes whatever is held on itself
by sand…

Soon their momentary togetherness comes to an
end,
when the wave returns back into the ocean
leaving sand at the other end…

On its way back, it also leaves behind beautiful
impressions on sand…
And keeps oscillating in rhythm, weaving
together water and land...

Gifts it pearls, shells and conches from ocean
bed to treasure…
Isn't this most amazing relationship going
smooth since forever ?!!

CONQUER

Been wondering, for quite some time now..
Who can ensure how my day goes and how?

We either take control of our day,
Or get carried through come what may…

When is this decided by the way?
In the early hours of morning, you can definitely
conquer your day…

Else get dragged all through the clock's typical
round way...
May you conquer your today, everyday!

MAGIC OF WORDS

Every single possible story,
Can be seen from perspectives many…
Someone's story is as clear as ice,
Someone's story sums up numerous lies...

Whom you trust and whom you won't do,
Depends on whose version of story you are
listening to...

Because it's the narration and not the fact,
which creates an impression and leaves an
impact...

Leading to the same old twisted confusion,
One caused by mind and heart's fusion…

Where mind readily accepts the fact,
but heart believes only what it feels is apt...

Such is the magic of word, action and sound,
Hence truth is often silent and pretence is loud…

In this never-ending game of truth and lies,
Believe only what you see with your own
eyes…

PHASES

Phases....of Light and of Darkness...
Phases....of Sunrises and of Sunsets...
Aren't they just like,
the phases in our lives?

Many of us who started together the same day,
are at different stages in life today…
and everyone's journey shall continue,
in its own distinct way....

While that being true, one can't really compare,
own course of journey with someone else out
there…

You never know whose phase is the brightest,
and who is struggling to get through the
darkest...

I see a similar equation between the Sun and the
Moon,
One fades by early morning other brightest at
noon…

One rises other sets, one sets other rises,
Both have their own defined phases…

And most importantly, both shine,
Only when it's their own 'Time'!!!

For any phase you might be in today,
be hopeful for a brighter day…

Where you shall be shining at your spectacular
best,
and so shall everything around do, to complete
the picture rest....

For anyone believing to be in their darkest,
Be assured of a phase, that will be your
brightest…

They say, nothing in our life can last forever,
Not even the darkest phase, so give up never!!!

OPPOSITES

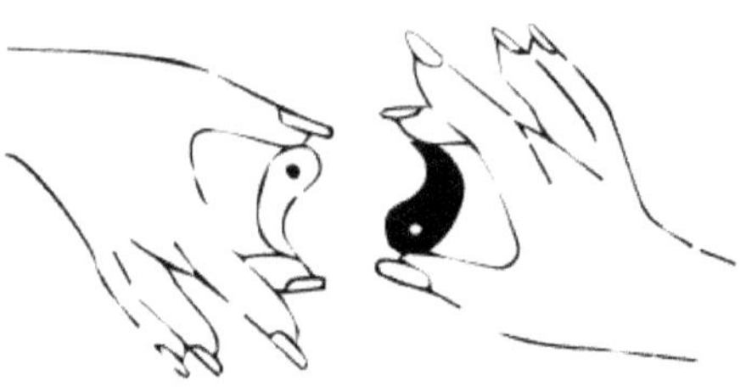

Saw two trees right beside each other,
Perhaps, ironically meant to be together…

One almost dried, dull, leafless..
Other lush green, lively, blooming freshness…

Both sharing common soil and similar weather...
Yet so distinct, wonder what made them differ?

Because it is not about what you receive,
Everything depends on how you receive!!

Good versus Evil,
God versus Devil…

Day versus Night,
Wrong versus Right…

Such opposites often exist together,
Probably for striking a balance in nature!

YOU NEED A REASON

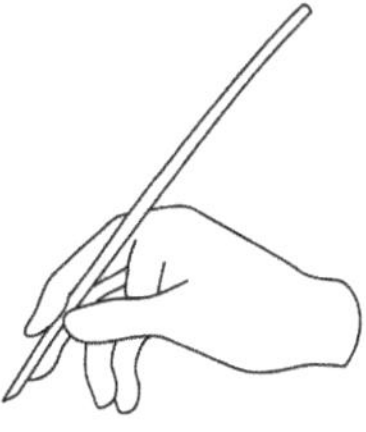

For someone 'hopeful',
To think and plan something unimaginable,
And not to believe in defined boundaries or
horizons,
Just needs a reason....

For someone 'joyful',
To smile at every shade of emotion, life takes
him through,
And not to sink in the depth of days dull and
blue,
Just needs a reason.....

For someone 'optimistic',
To see only "can do" out of "can't do",
And not to fall for that short "im-" before
"possible",
Just needs a reason.....

For someone 'loving',
To dance with a broken heart to the rhythm of
his beloved,
And not to let the worries of mind over-rule
silent desires of heart,
Just needs a reason.....

For an 'achiever',
To make a way out of all obstacles and travel
through to success,
And not to stop mid-way, no matter what the
journey takes,
Just needs a reason....

For someone 'responsible',
To observe and to take hold of the situation
observed,
And not to be a sufferer in silence when justice
is deserved,
Just needs a reason.....

For someone reading this,
To be any of the above,
And not to be either of the above,
You just need a reason....

May you choose your reason wisely today,
To become what you wish to be everyday....

MAGIC OF SOMEDAY

Walking solely through the lane,
Without any worry of loss or gain…

I remember, I was pretty much me,
until I saw him through the pane!

Just as the Earth revolves solely around the Sun,
Every year she follows the same orbit to finish
year one,

I saw the gleam which I wished to see,
Felt the magic which was very new to me!

With loads of memories and loads of smiles,
I looked for myself as I crossed the miles!

For the one who went was me,
But the one who came was just like me…

As everything ends so did that someday,
Would treasure it in my mind..as long as I may!!

ECLIPSE

Every being on the Earth is a unique creation,
Sharing with every other a different equation…

Some you cannot stand distant from,
Some you cannot get closer to…

Everyone is a combination of white and black,
Honing few good qualities, while several they
lack…

It all depends on how close you choose to be,
How influenced or uninfluenced you opt to be…

Some will hold you in place, just like the Sun
holds the Earth,
Some will calm you everyday, just like the
Moon calms the Earth…

Some will accompany you in the journey to
make you stronger,
Some will intensify your journey to make you
wiser…

Some will meet you for an Eclipse, once in a
year or few,
Some will challenge your skills daily, so you
upgrade to levels new…

Even if your worlds collide,
Never let your faith slide…

Even if you are overshadowed, it is for a while,
Don't let anyone take over your existence, or
dim your smile…

For your light exists by itself and shines out
bright,
While dark shadows exist only in the absence of
light…

Even in stages of Eclipse, hold your head
upright,
Soon it will end, making the world again witness
your might!

POSSIBILITY

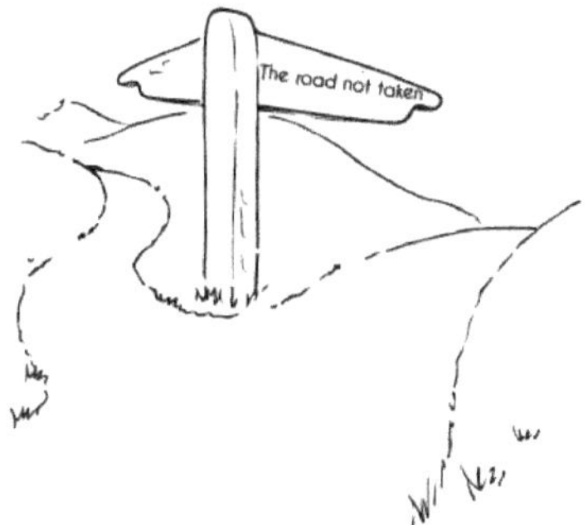

Possibilities can never be restricted,
So why should your imagination be?

Thoughts can never be limited,
So why should your vision be?

Capabilities can be limitless,
So why shouldn't your dreams be?

Life is not predictable,
So why should you be?

Difficulties are non-negotiable,
So why shouldn't your aspirations be?

The world is evolving everyday,
So why shouldn't you be?

Challenges are not repeated,
So how can your solutions be?

Your competitors are confident of your
strengths,
So how can you not be?

OWN YOUR FIGHT

While you juggle all the stuff, at once daily,
Take a moment to pause and straighten your
crown, dearly…

As there will be several compromises, coming
your way,
But when it comes to your self-worth, never let
it go that way…

Neither should you wait, for someone else to
pick up the baton,
To fight on your behalf, and to bring down
Satan…

Instead own your fight, by being as fearless as
you can,
Listen to your inner warrior, by being as
courageous as you can…

Let them judge, compare, comment and belittle
you,
Don't forget, the prettiest treasure your loved
ones have is you!

To the world, there may be so many like you,
To your dear ones, the whole world is only and
only you!

Know you are valued, know you are pretty,
Know you are worthy, never feel pity..

Your smile is precious, don't let anyone take it
away,
Just keep clearing the noise, and lead your path
to the top all the way!

ONE DAY

One day, the Sun shall shine brightest on you,
One day, the birds shall lovingly chirp for you…

Morning shall feel beautiful again,
Your struggles of today, won't go in vain…

And with the first few special sunrays, your face
shall glow,
While you dance your mind away, and sip your
tea slow…

That day shall explain a lot to you,
Why did life in first place challenge you?

How did you walk through the dark way up?
Why weren't you ever allowed to give up?

Everything comes with a price, and so would
that day..

Where you shall feel in control, all along the
day…

Such shall be the day, even peaceful shall be the
night,
Where you would exchange happiness, and
celebrate every aspect of life...

Who would ever need a vacation, from such a
day?
And who would mind living such a day,
everyday?!!!

GREY SCALE

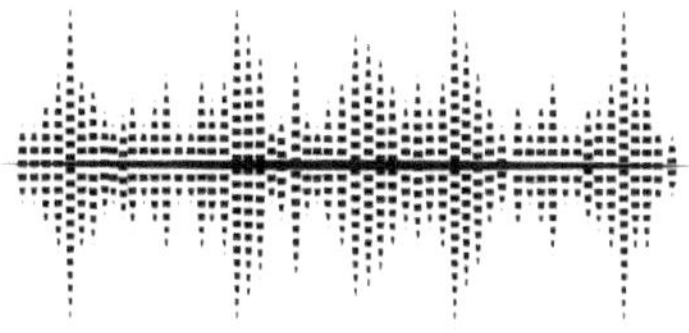

Sometimes, life turns on the grey scale mode,
Not too dull,
Not too bright…

Not fully dark,
Not fully light…
Just between the extremes of Black and White…

To keep up the balance,
To keep up the pace…
We choose to find peace,
and not race...

But deep in mind, let some hope survive,
That someday soon, life shall revive…

To bring back those hues,
To bring back that shade…
To bring back the rainbow,
whose colours won't fade...

LIKE SUN LIKE YOU

Different stages of life,
need different versions of You…
Like different hours of the day,
need different positioning of the Sun too…

Wherever You are,
You are meant to be!!!
On, above or beneath the horizon of Sea…

Making this world beautiful,
by just being You...
Changing everyday,
lesser like yesterday's, and more like today's
You!

BEST VERSION

Travelled kilometres to-n-fro for work by now,
But how many steps did you take towards You?

Must've exchanged several emojis since morning
on various apps we use,
But how many times did you look up and smile
in-real at You?

Chasing deadlines one after the other,
And setting new goals each day higher…
But did you ever set a due date for yourself,
To reach your own quota of carefree laughter??

Must've spared enough time to get several things
including your apps updated today,
But when was the last time you upgraded your
love for a hobby which you always wished to
pursue someday??

And now, for those who wish to change their
answers to the questions raised above few,
Do revise your schedule for tomorrow by adding
a criterion new—
Which may be named "me-time" and its sole aim
would be to chase the "best version of You!!!"

LITTLE THINGS

This beautiful tiny succulent makes me smile...
Little things can do that, if looked at for a
while!!

Those first few raindrops,
Those distant bright shining stars…

Those conches found on the beachside,
That melodious chirping of birds outside…

Are a few of the many joy-giving things around
us,
Available only, if you ignore worries and focus!

SUNSET

Sunset!
No matter how many times I see this view,
Yet each time it feels so stunning and new…

The closer you go, the more beautiful it is...
The clearer you see, the more blissful it is…

Gaze at the Sun, amaze at the reflections,
Forget mundane days, cherish God's creations!

Looking at the setting sun, reminds me of grace,
Though tomorrow it shall rise again, with a
powerful and bright face…

Living fully one day at a time, setting up your
own pace,
Respecting your own time and speed, not
rushing blindly through any race!

CYCLAMEN

On a lovely morning, with bright sunlight and
fresh air,
Sipping hot coffee, gave my plants a loving
stare…

Amidst them stood a Cyclamen beaming with
pure bliss,
With a perfectly structured arrangement, that one
couldn't miss…

And soon I wonder how it resembles the journey
of life so well,

At top stood the most mature flowers standing
steady upright,
Covering lovingly below them newly blooming
floret buds and leaves tight…

Last bending are the oldest flowers that lived it
all and are ready to fall,
Beneath them are roots holding and nourishing
through it all…

Isn't our life pretty much the same?
Going through such levels is also our game!

Those who are ready to conquer the world are
seldom at top you see,
Those who are still naive are at a level below,
learning how to fight to survive and be…

Ultimately the finishers descend down slow,
Leaving this world behind, with wisdom they
glow…

Rooting for us throughout are our values and
beliefs,
Some we are born with, some acquired, and
some learnt for relief…

Be it a cyclamen, or be it men,
All living entities follow this cycle the same!

Whatever level you are at,
Just keep giving your best with full heart…
As today you are the oldest you have ever been,
And also the youngest you will ever be!

JUST FLOW

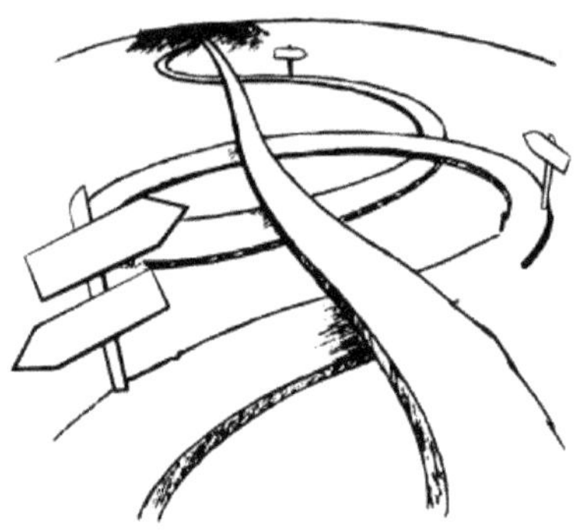

Yesterday you were there,
Today you are here…

Tomorrow you may reach far, or somewhere
near,
But you are growing each day, so don't doubt or
fear…

Overcoming obstacles, one after another,
Each new obstacle feels overpowering, until you
overpower…

No matter how the path is, just keep going, they
say...
Soon you will make the path yours, making
every way your way…

This is how a river keeps flowing for ages,
Discovering its own pathway in rigid mountain ranges…

Surpassing with persistence, whatever comes ahead,
Turning by its presence, mere land to a river bed…

Of course, river flows broadly at some points and narrowly in some region,
But it keeps flowing throughout, until it meets the ocean…

So don't stop on a tough day, keep going with the flow,
Some days you will run faster, on others a bit slow…

Mould your obstacles, or get moulded in the process,
Just keep flowing, until you arrive at your desired point of success!

SAME BUT DIFFERENT

There is so much you have seen,
but there is so much left to see…

For this world is so beautiful,
So varied, so rich, so bountiful...

No two days in your life are exactly the same,
But what you do each day is mostly the same!

Routine part of the day is made of mere cycles,
Remaining part of the day is what can lead you
to miracles!

You have changed in some aspects through the
years,
But in some, you are still the same old you!
Relook at every life pattern followed for years,
Everyday make time for learning something
new!

If you have arrived in life, great! Continue being
the same,
If you are yet to arrive in life, get started with
this wonderful game!

Be your own master, zero down on skills to ace,
Amplify your strengths, to increase chances of
winning this race!

This world is somewhat same as it was billions
of years before,
Yet it is so different from how it existed a billion
years before!

Choose what you should keep same,
Act on what you wish was different...
Otherwise day to day life remains the same,
until you create something different...

Don't live an entirely same pattern of day for
sixty years and call it a life,

Live each day to make some difference in sixty ways and lead a memorable life!

OVERCOME YOUR FEAR

One step at a time,
One stride a day…

One determined mind,
Self-motivated and kind…

That's all it takes for any journey or challenge
ahead,
No matter what pulls you back, don't bow down
your head…

Sure there will be storms, and thunders, and
rains,

But what good is a success, if achieved without
any pains?

If you are blessed with supporters, you have
already won half the battle,
If you just have yourself as a supporter, you are
fighting an even greater battle…

For your greatest strength is you,
Your biggest competitor is you…

Your greatest trust should be in yourself,
Don't sell yourself short, seek for higher self...
And then magic shall unfold, just as you wish to
see,
You are capable to climb any mountain, as long
as you believe to be…

Take that first step today,
Tick that box in to-do list today…

You have doubted yourself for long,
Don't stay anywhere you feel you don't belong…

You live only once, so do what matters to you...
Overcome your fear yourself, no one else can do
that for you!

SEASONS

Life is a combination of people, emotions, and
places,
Each place seems like a chapter, with same old
or new faces…

Constantly changing, often playful,
If it were a painting, it would be vibrantly
colourful!

Somedays are all about being happy, then some
days sad,
Somedays are worth celebrating, some days
quite bad…

Some phases of life, appear to be full of
uncertainty,
It then throws challenges your way, so you gain
some clarity!

When you feel you are losing it all, think it's
your cold winter or autumn,
When you feel you are winning it all, don't lose
your momentum…

Believe to aim for the sky, and use desire to fuel
your wing,
No season lasts forever, your autumn will be
soon replaced with summer, followed by spring!

FRAGRANCE OF FIRST RAIN

There is a strong connection,
between surrounding and emotion…

Some places bring out the best in you,
Some places you just feel aren't meant for you…

But there is always a place just a stroll away,
Where you can instantly feel at home, even if
away…

And that is amidst nature, with greenery around,
Where melodious chirping of birds, acts as a
calming sound…

That rhythmic flow of water, that fragrance of
first rain,
That soothing fresh breeze of air, that sight of
colourful flora unwinding your brain…

Those perfectly synced waves, dancing on the
shore,
Those rare warm sun rays in winter, warming
your core…

Those lovely shiny stars, lighting up the night
sky,
Those precious dew drops in the morning not
letting the leaves dry…

That magnificent symmetry of flowers,
Those tall coconut trees like towers…

Timely connect with them and recharge yourself,
Soak in the pure air time to time, and rejuvenate
yourself!

STAND ON YOUR OWN FEET

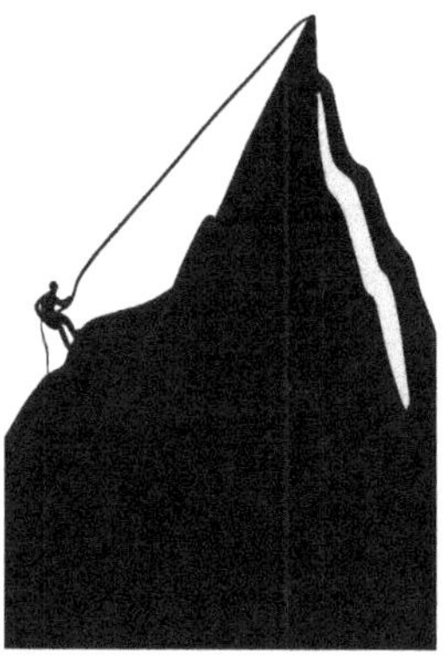

Don't follow the crowd blindly, you will seldom
meet yourself there,
Don't fall into the trap of herds, you will never
elevate yourself there…

If you wish to live a life different from them,
How will you reach your goal by following
them?

Devise your plan, learn through your errors,
Own up your responsibility, ignore the
talebearers…

You have come alone,
You shall leave alone…

What you do in between, is the real game,
Don't copy anyone else, earn your own name!

Because you are yourself, you are not them,
Your desires are unique, so how can your paths
be the same?

Everyone has limitations, you would too,
Work on your positives, acknowledge your
negatives too…

It's fine if you are late, at least now you can
begin,
Better late than never, you still have a chance to
win…

Stand on your own feet, they will never let you
down,
Take pride in your individuality, wear your own
crown…

Take inspiration from a mountain, standing firm
by itself,
Whatever calamities it faces, never gives up on
self…

Some landslide here and there, some weathering
is inevitable,
That's how one transforms in life, making this
journey memorable!

NEST MAKING STORY

Home is where the heart is,
Home is where comfort is…

Home is where you never pretend,
Home is where love doesn't end…

Home is made by you, for you,
Home is where your heart rests, be it old or
new…

Be it a beach-facing bungalow,
Be it a small cute nest..
While creating it you will always fall in love,
Like a bird does while building its nest...

We collect resources, birds collect sticks,
They don't think of outcomes every time, nor
about the risks…

Every rain makes the bird change its shelter,
Still, it never gets tired or lets its enthusiastic
spirit alter…

Birds keep changing places one after the other,
But they keep making beautiful nests everytime
better than previous other…
No one knows how many times they make it and
break it all,
But what keeps them going is not giving up on
their hardworking nature at all…

Come what may, build from scratch everyday,
No matter how many times you fail, you will
also make your dream home one day!

PARENTING

There is no joy greater than raising your
offspring,
For it's a chance to relive your childhood,
differently while parenting...

Don't seek for perfection,
Just soak it in as much as you can...
Don't give anyone justification,
Living it to the fullest should be your only plan!

Those tiny little eyes, see the world through you,
Those tiny little feet will soon learn to run past
you...

That little bundle of joy,
Soon becomes your favourite toy…
You forget what life was before,
You wonder, if you ever felt love of this kind
before!

Dance together in the rains,
Walk together through the trails…
Finish those ice cream cups soon,
Because their childhood also melts soon...

Parenting a teenager requires a different version
from your end,
Along with being a parent, now you also need to
become your child's best friend!

Every parent in nature loves young one with all
their heart,
Providing whatever is possible in their capacity,
while fulfilling every part!

And babies have a wonderful way of loving you
back,
They know no matter what, their parents always
have their back!

MAKING MEMORIES

You still remember your childhood favourites,
That strawberry ice cream and those chocolate
milkshakes…

Those curious visits to parks, and zoos and
beaches,
Those weekend road trips starting with yummy
sandwiches…

Running to catch hold of the beautiful
butterflies,
Tracing back source of rain by chasing raindrops
with wide eyes…

Making cute small handmade greeting cards,
Creatively scribbling all over house walls…

Learning to swim, skate, and run,
Childhood days were mostly fun…

Then came your high school days,
Night-outs, picnics and coffee dates…

And so on life continues, from stage to stage,
While we unknowingly make memories for our
albums page to page..

But the nature that time was different from the
nature today,
It was way more pure, and so much less polluted
than today…

Seasons were predictable,
Global warming was avoidable…

Today we don't have that luxury,
That pure untouched nature is just a memory!!

LIFE IS A JUNGLE

Life is just like a Jungle,
Combination of stability, adventure and
upheaval!

You likely have a loving clan,
Whom you can always count on and plan…

But there are others too fighting for the crown,
With whom you may not get along with a smile
or a frown…

Amongst the same group, there is constantly an
unsaid race,
To stay ahead, you need to run faster in order to
win the race…

There can only be one king of this jungle too,
Let it be your intellect, who can work for you or
against you too!

Trust everyone around, but be the sole decision
maker...
Decisions can never let you lose if you are
determined to be kingmaker…

Everyone leaves back traces, so shall you,
Do something valuable for your kingdom to
remember, after you leave the jungle too!

EVOLVE AS YOU BREATHE

What good are you if you are just like yesterday,
even today?
If you are willing to grow, won't you need to
upscale today?

Different outcomes that you dream of,
Need a different version of you too…
Don't correct your mistakes as a tradeoff,
Evolve in the process too!

Evolving needs effort as walking an extra mile,
With one good habit a day, or one positive
thought a while…

The more you evolve, the more you see,
How naive were you before, how evolved you
could be!

Growing through the odds will give you real
satisfaction,
Working on yourself will give you everlasting
motivation!

This is your story, take charge to make it
worthwhile,
Edit, delete and reword as you need, to keep it
agile!

Don't only do the usual,
Don't always keep it casual…

Evolve with every passing breath,
Let your success story be the most valuable asset
you ever bequeath!

FORCE ABOVE

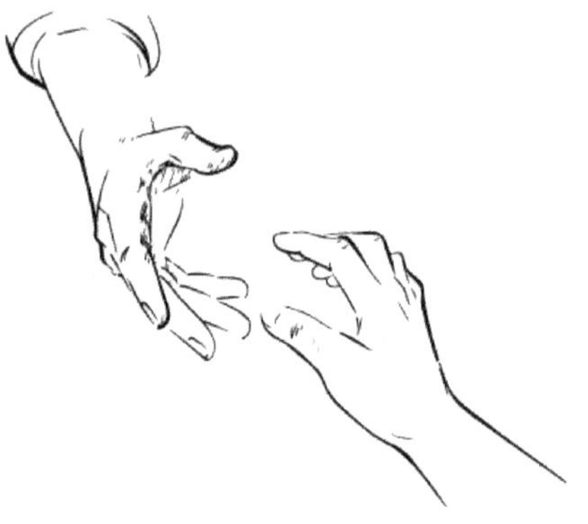

So many planets in the solar system,
Who keeps them in position and how?

So many stars in the Milky Way,
Who holds each star in place and how?

So many gravitation pulls on Earth,
Who balances it and how?

So many creatures in our world,
Who ensured their survival and how?

Who teaches the birds to fly?
How do they know to aim at the sky?

Who teaches fish how to breathe underwater?
Who taught man why he needs to have a shelter?

There has to be a force greater, watching
somewhere from above,
Who holds us all together, before whom most of
us bow!

Right from the Big Bang until today,
This force keeps life in motion, running
smoothly everyday…
Destruction might be easy,
Creation is complicated…
All creatures are so different,
Yet evolutionarily related…

Such is the magic of our Creator,
Who visualised it all and got us through...
Only he knows the fate of our Earth better,
Or is he already busy creating another Earth
anew?

GOODNESS FLOWS BACK

Always keep doing good, as one should,
But never expect it in return, nor hope it
would…

For having a pure heart is like keeping a clean
slate,
Goodness is bound to return, either early or
late...

Don't think the grass is greener on that side,
Or that the grass is lesser on your side,
Grass is greener wherever it is watered,
Be it your side or that side...

Jealousy, hatred, and obsession are toxic traits to
name a few,
Don't compare yourself with others because no
one else is you!

Your strengths and weaknesses are a unique
combination,
No one can alter it but you, so never lose your
motivation...

Keep walking the right path,
Even if it takes longer...
Don't fall for the short path,
In which you may reach your end point earlier
but still wander...

Kindness and empathy are rare to find today,
If you find them in someone, treasure them as
angelic souls today...

Keep sharing goodness, for wide smiles
spanning from ear to ear,
Mother nature has been doing this for us, year
after year...

Someday someone will be out there,
Who will take note and replenish your due
share…

Who will make you believe how right were you,
And why the world needs more goodness
flowing from people like you...

SPRING

Aren't you smiling a bit more today?
Are your eyes gleaming for no reason?
You are dancing to your own tune today,
As if it is your personal spring season!

Opting for dynamic and vibrant colours,
Which otherwise won't see light of the day,
Checking out yourself so much in mirrors,
Looking like rejuvenating sunshine today!

You are blooming and blushing,
Exactly as plants do in spring…

How beautiful is this warm and earthy air,
Even peacocks know it's time to let down hair!

Soon rains will shower abundance and cheer,
Spreading the magic of raindrops rhythm in your
ear…

The charm of fresh colourful flowers, and cosy
warmth are just few reasons,
Why spring is my most favourite, out of all
seasons!

ADAPT

If you cannot run, walk...
If you cannot walk, crawl...

If you cannot find abundance, create...
If you cannot grow, migrate...

For every adversity,
Can be overcome with adaptability...

Adapt to your surroundings,
Adapt for your longings...

Adapting is the law of nature,
For survival of the fittest and not amateur...

Original you, may not be able to do the
impossible,

But adapted you can turn every impossible into possible...

SYMMETRY

Did you ever realise?
The symmetry of your eyes...

There is beauty in everything that nature has...
There is a uniform symmetry in everything
nature has…

Look at the veins on leaves,
Look at the wings of the bees…

Look at the petals of flowers,
Look at the drops in rain showers…

Look how perfectly shaped are the fruits of each
plant,
Look how perfectly layered are the seeds of each
plant…

Look at the engravings on the oyster shells,
Look at the textures of the coconut shells,,,

Look at the stripes on tigers and zebras,
Look at the colourful patterns on peacocks and
giraffes…

So much like one another,
yet so much different than the other…

Marvelling at how precisely nature creates,
Encoding each creation so that it exactly
replicates...

Symmetry is the basis of our existence,
Maintained by nature since forever with
persistence…

THE NEW RICH

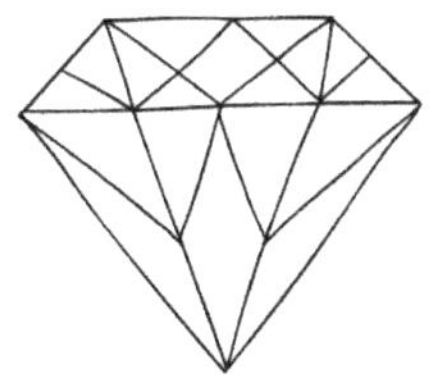

The new rich is unlike the conventional rich in
many different ways,
It is not just earning that matters, what you earn
as wealth is the case!

Being healthy is the biggest luxury one could
ever have,
Staying healthy is the biggest feat one could
ever achieve…

In this era of growing social media attention,
Virtual world is taking over real social
interaction…

Having success by yourself is great,
But having someone to celebrate your success
with, is way more great…

Eating clean,
Not being mean…

Saving only a fat bank balance,
While keeping yourself lean…

Spending time doing meditation,
Will keep you away from antidepressants or
similar medication…

Devouring organic and fresh nature produce,
Devising new solutions for pollution to reduce…

Not cutting down forests for endless selfish use,
But planting trees responsibly for future
generations to use…

Not being a cause of anyone's depression,
And being the source of someone's inspiration!

Looking young only by staying fit,
Living in harmony with nature and not against
it!

TIME TRANSFORMS EVERYTHING

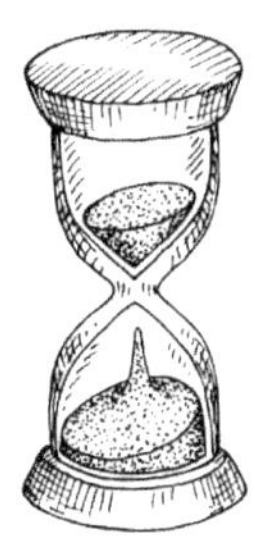

What was once a tiny seed,
is now a huge and widespread tree…

What was once a sturdy rock,
has now weathered to sand, on which we walk…

Once these rocks and stones were so rough,
But flowing river water from above made them
smooth on outside and kept inside tough…

What all it took to change them?
Nothing, just time gradually transformed them!

We humans are no different, we age with time
too,
Don't resist and let time do its magic on you
too…

You are not how you were born, with every
passing moment time is transforming you,
If you acknowledge and embrace the fact, you
shall soon realise, you are time's masterpiece
too!

WHO SAYS MAGIC DOESN'T HAPPEN?

You barely notice it sometimes,
But it happens much more often!
Magic is everywhere around us,
If only one could observe and learn…

Else how do the stars several light years away,
Appear on your night sky as if they are here to
forever stay,

And how do the northern lights,
Dance as spectacular auroras at selective nights?

And how is a tiny seed,
capable of becoming a giant Banyan tree?

If magic doesn't happen,
How would fireflies on their own illuminate?
Shining in the dark with a mystic aura they
create…

And how would even the glow-worms know,
When it's time to be luminous and glow?

Magic surely exists,
It always has...
Magic is in the evolution,
Magic is in daily rotation of the Earth and its
annual revolution,

Magic is everyone's favourite hope,
When logic is over and there is no further
scope…

The word "magic" itself brings smiles,
Suddenly sparkling shine in otherwise gloomy
eyes…

Magic is everywhere and still nowhere,
All you need is to believe in it and it is just away
a stare!

PURE

Purity is in the soul of nature,
Purity is the essence of nature…

The melting glaciers give purest water to the
river,
The river runs several miles to bring us water
pure…

Pure is the honey,
Collected by bees many…

Pure are the dewdrops,
Appearing on leaves in morning as the
temperature drops…

Pure is the love between a baby and its mother,

Pure is the loyalty between a pet and its
keeper…

Pure is this Mother Earth and we live in this
heaven,
Which keeps giving us so much more, even if so
much is already given!

FLAMINGOS

Quietly walking in the forest by the lakeside,
Suddenly with excitement, my eyes went open
wide,

As I saw a flamboyance of flamingos taking
flight...
Watching those mesmerising hues of pink
feathers is truly a delight…

Blissfully, they were enjoying light showers and
weather...
Each one monitoring the surroundings and
keeping an eye for safety of one another…

Some making a queue, knowingly or
unknowingly while they walk,
Some chirping indistinctly as if lovingly they
could talk…

Some flamingoes love to dance,
Some look down at water with a focused
glance...

What amazed me most was their sense of unity,
As they are committed to keeping everyone safe
in the community...
Watching such a beautiful flamboyance was an
experience like never before,
Even hundreds of pictures aren't enough to
capture them in memories to store...

Allowing me to watch from a distance, they
were supportive and kind...
As if all this was another teaching from nature,
for me to learn and unwind...

COUNT YOUR BLESSINGS

Grateful for the air I breathe,
Grateful for the land beneath,

Grateful for this chance to live,
Grateful for the blessing of God in whom I
believe...

Grateful for every person in my life,
Who knowingly and unknowingly teaches me
lessons for life…

Grateful for the surprises, shocks, and
challenges,
Which lead to significant and transformative life
changes...

Don't just count your difficulties,
Without focusing on your blessings...
Remember you can overcome any calamities,

By seeking guidance from God's and nature's teachings...

RAINBOW

Loads and loads of laughter,
Some tears of happiness and some of sadness
after…

Tons and tons of excitement,
Also a bit of humble acknowledgement…

Endless series of neverending adventures,
Massive motivation after failures, to restart with
new ventures…

Limitless abundant flow of love,
Sheer joy, and enthusiasm of a flying dove…

Inevitable fear, anger, and hatred,
To be kept minimum and channelised into
positivity like a trade…

All these are emotions of life through which you flow,
But you need all of them to witness a complete rainbow!

A bit of Violet, a pinch of Indigo, and a lot of warm Blue,
A hopeful Green, a little mellow Yellow, a vibrant Orange and a fiery Red too!

All these colours come harmoniously together,
And form a rainbow in the presence of each other…

Similarly, it takes every emotion, to live life to its best,
Don't let any one emotion overpower you for long or hinder the emotions rest!

SET YOUR HORIZON

Everything in the world is expected to be black
or white,
Can we really categorise everything as wrong or
right?

The boundaries are not as clear as night
and day,
Because in real, things aren't fully white or fully
black—but grey,

And so.. your right, is not quite right for me,
And your wrong, is not that wrong for me…

There is always a blurred thin borderline,
Hence your horizon is different from mine…

Let's not force each other to push our horizons,
Mind our own thing and keep healthy
boundaries intact for many reasons!

Horizon is like a mirage, not definite but
existing,
But you need it to differentiate between your
personal right and wrong setting…

If you are authentic, your conscience will tell
you each time,
How to set your horizon, so you do justice with
your true self every time…

YOU HEAL YOU

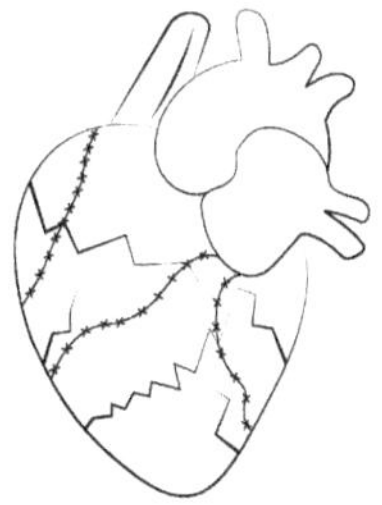

What is a true sign of progressing in life?
Some scars visible and some invisible-like…

Some get healed on their own in really no time,
Some need your effort for healing well in time...

There is no scar that you can't heal by yourself,
Just close your eyes and believe in yourself…

Say aloud, I am much more stronger than this
scar or wound to sore,
I can heal myself through this too, as I have
several times before...

Don't heal for anyone else's sake,
Heal for your well-being and happiness sake…

Don't wait for anyone else to check on you,
It is your first responsibility towards yourself to
heal you...

YOUR MIND YOUR GARDEN

Your mind is like your garden,
Which you nurture as per your vision…

What you wish to reap,
is what exactly you need to sow...
Give it fertilisers of joy and happiness,
And regularly remove weeds of sorrow…

Use your words and actions to shape it carefully,
And water your garden with good thoughts to
moisten it appropriately…

Protect your garden well from rampant
infestations,
Of negativity, jealousy, anger, hatred, and unjust
accusations…

Focus on your parameters of self-growth,
To get a good harvest of success and
contentment, both…

Stay vigilant of what seeds every day you sow,
Because only those will occupy your mind space
and endlessly grow…

ULTIMATE BOND

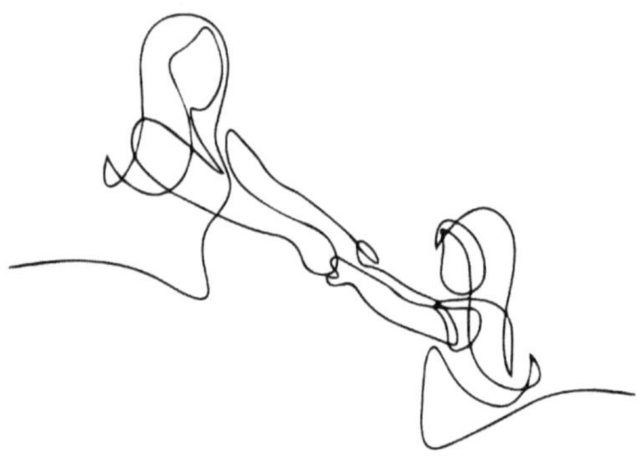

For some, you are always a bit more,
For some, you are always a bit less…

For some, you are quite bitter,
For some, you are much sweeter...

Let the ever-changing world change opinion
about you everyday,
Because to your child you are the entire
WORLD everyday!!!

There is no bond more pure, more natural, or
fulfilling,
Than the bond shared between a mother and her
offspring!

I thought I knew my capabilities before
becoming a mother,
But I am only getting to know my strengths after
being a mother...

Eternally grateful to my mother for giving me
this life,
Eternally grateful to my baby for becoming my
life....

Such is the bond between every mother and
offspring,
Be it a baby, a kitten, a calf, or a cub of the lion
king!

FRIENDSHIP

If one wishes to walk fast and far,
One can definitely walk by oneself...
But if one wishes to walk happily and far,
One should walk with a friend of self…

Friend is like your companion not exactly in
your shoes,
But who looks at the world through you, as if in
your shoes!

Someone who likes you not just at your best,
But also lends a strong shoulder on tough days
to rest…

One with whom you can be your truest self,
Who will not judge your mistakes, yet make you
reflect on self…

Someone who cheers exclusively for you,
Someone who sheds happy tears for you…

Some friendships are short-lived,
Some are meant to be so special and
long-lived…

It is a blessing to celebrate life with good
friends!
If friendship is genuine it lasts forever, never
ends…

True friendship is indeed a priceless bond to
share,
Most meaningful when both you and your friend
truly care...

YOU ARE NOT WHAT THEY TELL YOU

You are not what people think about you,
You are not what people demand from you…

You are not what others spread about you,
You are not what others speak about you...

Whenever in doubt, always look within,
Seek validation about yourself, only from
within,

You do not need to prove anything to anyone,
And remember, it's not at all necessary to be
liked by everyone!

Live with your constants but live for yourself
too,
Live with those around whom you feel safe,
happy and celebrated too…

There will always be someone out, passing false
notions about you,
Even if in reality that someone knows absolutely
nothing about you...

You are not what they tell you,
Only you know who exactly are you!

Let critics criticise, let judges judge you,
Be your own critic, and believe only your own
judgement about you!

MANIFEST NOW!

We all dream of several things, day in and day
out,
Because there is always a deep desire to make it
big and somehow stand out...

Dreaming alone doesn't assure fulfilment,
Planning each step to fulfil your dream is the
real key to achievement...

But before you receive something,
You should feel worthy enough to have it!
Affirm yourself you are deserving,
And begin to manifest as if you have it!

Believe in the presence and existence of your
dream in near life,
Because manifestation is a magical wand that
often translates dreams into real life...